SPOTLIGHT ON OUR FUTURE

EQUALITY, SOCIAL JUSTICE, AND OUR FUTURE

SABRINA ADAMS

NEW YORK

Published in 2022 by The Rosen Publishing Group, Inc.
29 East 21st Street, New York, NY 10010

Copyright © 2022 by The Rosen Publishing Group, Inc.

All rights reserved. No part of this book may be reproduced in any form without permission in writing from the publisher, except by a reviewer.

First Edition

Editor: Theresa Emminizer
Book Design: Michael Flynn

Photo Credits: Cover Hero Images/Getty Images; (series background) jessicahyde/Shutterstock.com; p. 5 Anderson Ross Photography Inc/DigitalVision/Getty Images; p. 6 https://commons.wikimedia.org/wiki/File:Declaration_of_Independence_(1819),_by_John_Trumbull.jpg; p. 7 Hulton Archive/Getty Images; p. 8 Stringer/AFP/Getty Images; p. 9 https://commons.wikimedia.org/w/index.php?title=File:Eleanor_Roosevelt_UDHR.jpg&oldid=387677480; p. 11 -/Stringer/AFP/Getty Images; p. 13 Bryan R. Smith/AFP/Getty Images; p. 14 Bloomberg/Getty Images; p. 15 Cole Bennetts/Getty Images; p. 17 Rawpixel.com/Shutterstock.com; p. 18 Buyenlarge/Archive Photos/Getty Images; p. 19 Joseph Sohm/Shutterstock.com; p. 20 Kobby Dagan/Shutterstock.com; p. 21 Salvatore Di Nofi/Keystone/AP Images; p. 23 The Washington Post/Getty Images; p. 24 Barcroft Media/Getty Images; p. 25 Manish Swarup/AP/Getty Images; p. 26 fotosparrow/Shutterstock.com; p. 27 Gopen Rai/AFP/Getty Images; p. 29 Sia Kambou/AFP/Getty Images.

Cataloging-in-Publication Data

Names: Adams, Sabrina.
Title: Equality, social justice, and our future / Sabrina Adams.
Description: New York : PowerKids Press, 2022. | Series: Spotlight on our future | Includes glossary and index.
Identifiers: ISBN 9781725323940 (pbk.) | ISBN 9781725323971 (library bound) | ISBN 9781725323957 (6 pack)
Subjects: LCSH: Equality--Juvenile literature. | Social justice--Juvenile literature.
Classification: LCC HM821.A33 2022 | DDC 305--dc23

Manufactured in the United States of America

Some of the images in this book illustrate individuals who are models. The depictions do not imply actual situations or events.

CPSIA Compliance Information: Batch #CSPK22. For further information contact Rosen Publishing, New York, New York at 1-800-237-9932.

CONTENTS

SOCIAL JUSTICE FOR ALL 4

HUMAN RIGHTS. 6

A PUSH FOR CHANGE. 8

WOMEN'S RIGHTS MOVEMENTS 10

EQUALITY AMONG GENDERS 12

RIGHTS FOR THE LGBTQ COMMUNITY 14

ONE RACE. 16

FIGHTING RACISM. 18

UNDERSTANDING ETHNICITY 20

FREEDOM OF RELIGION 22

CLIMATE CHANGE AND SOCIAL JUSTICE. 24

EQUAL RIGHTS FOR PEOPLE WITH DISABILITIES 26

A SUSTAINABLE FUTURE. 28

A CHANGE FOR GOOD. 30

GLOSSARY 31

INDEX 32

PRIMARY SOURCE LIST 32

WEBSITES. 32

CHAPTER ONE

SOCIAL JUSTICE FOR ALL

Social justice is the idea that all people should have the same rights and opportunities and be treated fairly. No matter their race, **gender**, origin, religion, or ability, all people deserve these things.

Social justice takes hard work from the members of a society. People must bring unjust laws to the attention of court systems and lawmakers. **Activists** in social justice movements of the past and present have played a big part in accomplishing these goals.

Equality and equity are key ideas of social justice. Equality is equal treatment under the law and equal rights and opportunities. Equity, however, relates to equal outcomes as well. It takes into account different abilities and **privileges** in order to work toward equal outcomes for all. Social justice puts equality and equity into action.

While equality says all people have the right to enter a public building, equity provides the means to make it possible for everyone.

CHAPTER TWO

HUMAN RIGHTS

The idea of equality isn't a new one. It's grown and changed slowly throughout history. For most of human history, society has been organized with strict systems of power. Some systems were based on the belief that some people were naturally better than others. Upper classes had greater power and **resources**.

SIGNING OF THE DECLARATION OF INDEPENDENCE

Sometimes, fighting for rights can get bloody, such as during the French and American revolutions.

Over time, however, people began to consider the idea of human rights. Great thinkers spoke and wrote of the idea that people had the right to change society. A number of **revolutionary** movements started in the 1700s. The American colonies fought for freedom from Britain. Americans wrote a Declaration of Independence, voicing the idea that citizens have rights. Citizens created a similar declaration in France. In the 19th century, more nations fought for independence and the ideals of equality.

CHAPTER THREE
A PUSH FOR CHANGE

The struggle for equality for many groups increased in the late 1800s. In the years leading up to that time, the use of new machines drew people to work in city factories rather than farms. Many of these workers were treated poorly, and gaps between society classes grew. Injustices caused reformers, or people who push for changes to improve society, to act. Reformers pushed for laws to improve conditions in factories and housing projects.

ASSEMBLY OF THE UNITED NATIONS, 1948

Eleanor Roosevelt was a First Lady of the United States. She was part of the group that wrote the UN Declaration of Human Rights.

After World War II, world leaders formed the United Nations. This is an organization of nations that works toward peace and human rights. In 1948, the group created a list of common rights of all people around the world. Today, 192 nations have signed the declaration. However, people around the world still face inequalities because of their race, religion, and other differences.

CHAPTER FOUR
WOMEN'S RIGHTS MOVEMENTS

Across the globe, women have often historically been considered unequal to men. In many countries and times, women couldn't vote, hold office, or own property.

Activists led women's suffrage, or right to vote, movements to fight for greater equality. New Zealand, Australia, Finland, and Norway were the first countries to grant women suffrage. After World War I, 28 other countries gave voting rights to women, and more followed after World War II. In the United States, women won the right to vote in 1920.

Women's rights movements have helped create better opportunities for women. However, men still earn more money than women, even when they do the same work. Around the world, women make about 77 cents for every dollar a man makes. Women also don't have equal positions in governments as leaders and lawmakers.

New Zealand allowed women to vote starting in 1893. In Saudi Arabia, shown here, women were able to vote for the first time in 2015.

CHAPTER FIVE

EQUALITY AMONG GENDERS

Education is a powerful tool for improving women's lives. However, in many countries, girls aren't offered equal education. About 132 million girls around the world are currently out of school. For gender equality to exist, boys and girls need equal access, or ability to get to, quality schools.

CLINTON GLOBAL INITIATIVE, 2016

When Memory Banda (right) was just 13 years old, she took a stand against child marriage in her home country of Malawi.

Calling attention to gender equity problems is an important step in fixing them. Once a problem is understood, communities can take action. In Malawi, Memory Banda convinced her village to end **cultural** practices that hurt girls after her 11-year-old sister was forced to marry. Her story and activism helped many others. In 2017, Malawi outlawed child marriage. Child marriage contributes to health and education problems for girls. Banda and others continue to fight for an end to child marriage worldwide.

CHAPTER SIX

RIGHTS FOR THE LGBTQ COMMUNITY

The fight for gender equality is about more than just women's rights. It also includes the lesbian, gay, bisexual, transgender, and queer (LGBTQ) community. Social justice movements for the LGBTQ community try to end discrimination, or unfair treatment, including laws and other practices. Worldwide, LGBTQ people are discriminated against in terms of housing, education, employment, and health-care rights. Over one-third of the world's countries make being LGBTQ a crime. That means that people can be jailed because of whom they love.

In social movements around the world, the rainbow flag is a symbol of LGBTQ pride. In this gathering in Australia in 2017, an activist shows his support for legalizing same-sex marriage.

Activists are working to change the laws. They also help people understand LGBTQ issues and speak out against **violence** against LGBTQ people. This is an important part of ensuring social justice. Even in places where people are protected by the law, they often face social discrimination.

CHAPTER SEVEN

ONE RACE

People may be born with different skin colors, hair types, and facial features. Many people inherit, or are born with, features that are passed on by their family members. For centuries, people with certain shared traits, or features, have been grouped together into races. These traits aren't important in and of themselves. They're just things some societies decided were important.

People are more alike than different. The Human Genome Project was an important partnership between scientists around the world. They worked together to map, or study, the genes of people from around the world. The project was launched in 1990 and completed in 2003. It proved just how alike all humankind is. Unfortunately, race has been and is still used as reason for treating people unjustly.

The genes that make up any two humans are always at least 99.9 percent the same.

CHAPTER EIGHT

FIGHTING RACISM

Racism is the idea that some races are better than others. This idea has caused inequality and injustice throughout the world.

Both the United States and South Africa have had examples of **legalized** racism. Both countries enforced strict separations between black and white citizens and discrimination against black citizens. In response, modern civil rights movements demanded equality. These movements were successful in creating stronger legal protections for black people. However, social and cultural discrimination still exists around the world.

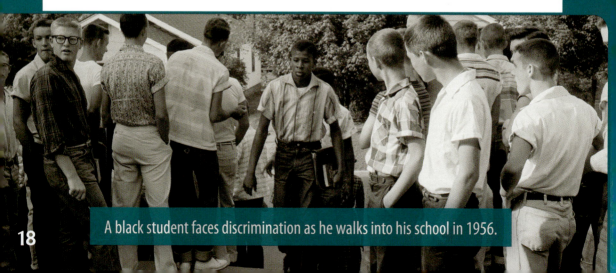
A black student faces discrimination as he walks into his school in 1956.

Speaking up against racist ideas, words, and actions is one way to work toward equality.

Racism targets more than just black communities. Racial groups around the world experience the effects of racism in different ways. No matter what race you identify with, establishing racial equality is everyone's responsibility. New movements against racism continue to raise people's awareness and demand fairness for people of all races.

CHAPTER NINE

UNDERSTANDING ETHNICITY

An ethnicity is a group of people who share common cultural traits. Language, religion, and more all make ethnic groups different from each other.

People of different nations and races can share ethnicity. For example, Hispanic ethnicity includes people in many nations with a shared language. At the same time, multiple ethnicities can exist within one country. For example, Brazil alone has hundreds of different cultural groups. Among those groups there are many different languages. People have their own ethnic identities that are distinct from each other and from other Brazilians.

Hamangaí Pataxó of Brazil, shown here, has worked to protect the rights of local ethnic groups since she was a teenager. In 2019, she addressed the Young Activists Summit in Geneva, Switzerland.

Ethnic conflicts have occurred throughout the world. Many result in violence, discrimination, and forced assimilation. Assimilation means blending in with the customs of a group. However, multicultural societies that respect their many parts can be a strong model for other nations.

CHAPTER TEN

FREEDOM OF RELIGION

The ability to practice your chosen religion is an important right. More than 84 percent of the world's population is part of a religious group. However, many people are treated unfairly because of their beliefs.

Some governments limit religious practices. They may do this through laws, policies, or military actions. For example, France made it illegal for women to wear a **burka** in public. Social discrimination affects some religious groups. Individuals may be **harassed** for their religious dress. Religious groups are sometimes targeted in terror attacks.

The United Nations has created programs to protect religious freedom around the world. One program promotes education and understanding about respecting different religions. Another program protects holy sites around the world. This helps keep the places where people worship safe.

Hana Kaur Mangat was 12 when she helped found Sikh Kid 2 Kid in Maryland. She helped teach adults about her Sikh religion.

CHAPTER ELEVEN

CLIMATE CHANGE AND SOCIAL JUSTICE

A migrant is a person who moves from one place to another, often in search of better living conditions or work. Throughout history, people have migrated for different reasons. Today, about 65.3 million people have been forced to leave their homes because of conflict or **disaster**.

Climate change is one of the main reasons today that people have been forced from their homes. Storms, floods, and long dry periods called droughts make areas hard to live in. People lose homes, jobs, and safety because of climate change.

ACTIVISTS AT THE GLOBAL CLIMATE MARCH IN BANGLEDESH, 2015

In September 2019, Pandey joined 15 other young activists in suing five countries. The activists claim the countries fail to protect children from the effects of climate change.

Activist Ridhima Pandey takes the issue of climate change seriously. Pandey lives in Uttarakhand, India, where floods and landslides have deadly effects. She's also seen pollution and deforestation in India. Young people like Pandey are pushing for renewable energy **technologies** to help fight climate change.

CHAPTER TWELVE

EQUAL RIGHTS FOR PEOPLE WITH DISABILITIES

About 15 percent of the world's population lives with some kind of disability. Because disabilities often prevent people from working, these people are twice as likely to live in poverty.

Starting in the 1960s, many people in the United States fought to help bring attention to the problems of those with disabilities. This resulted in the Americans with Disabilities Act of 1990. The law protects the rights of people with disabilities. It also pushes for fairness in terms of access to buildings. Wheelchair ramps and parking spaces are examples of fairer access.

DisasterHack is a company that makes 3-D printed prostheses, or man-made limbs, for people hurt in disasters. The company will give this prosthetic hand to someone who couldn't afford it on their own.

Creative technologies can also help people with disabilities. Printing 3-D limbs can help people get access to these useful tools. Smart glasses can help some people see shades and colors. These technologies help people become more independent and active.

CHAPTER THIRTEEN

A SUSTAINABLE FUTURE

Inequality occurs in all countries. It happens in the least developed and the most developed nations. People need to pay attention to global issues as well as local issues. That's because these issues are interconnected throughout the world.

In the world today, the bottom 50 percent of the population has less than 10 percent of the world's wealth. This gap is getting bigger. This prevents economic growth and may cause social and political inequality. In the future, countries may have to look toward sustainable development, or the idea that decisions and policies should consider the present and the future. People in some countries may have to change their ways of thinking so that society supports all members and not just the wealthy few.

The world produces enough food to feed all of humankind, but one-third of this food is wasted. More than 800 million people are underfed.

CHAPTER FOURTEEN

A CHANGE FOR GOOD

Challenge yourself to learn more about equality and social justice. Interest in social justice can lead you toward a career in law or social work. There are many ways you can do your part. Remember, activists are ordinary people. They made a choice to help people in need. You can make that choice too.

Start small in your own community. Pay attention to issues of inequality. Listen to the people who are most affected. Encourage government leaders to adopt policies that support and protect people in need.

You can push for change on a global scale too. Get involved with international groups that push for equality. Read about leaders and activists who have goals similar to yours. The more you know, the more you will be able to help our global community.

GLOSSARY

activist (AK-tih-vist) Someone who acts strongly in support of or against an issue.

burka (BUR-kuh) A garment worn by some Muslim women that covers the entire body with a veiled opening for the eyes.

cultural (KUHL-chuh-ruhl) Having to do with the beliefs, practices, and arts of a group of people.

disaster (dih-ZAS-tuhr) Something that happens suddenly and causes much suffering and loss for many people.

gender (JEN-duhr) The set of social expectations or traits men or women are expected to meet or have.

harass (huh-RASS) To create a hostile or unpleasant situation for someone through unwanted contact.

legalized (LEE-guh-liyz) To make something legal, or allowed by law.

privilege (PRIHV-lij) A special advantage granted only to a particular person or group.

resource (REE-sohrs) A usable supply of something.

revolutionary (reh-vuh-LOO-shuh-nehr-ee) Relating to a revolution, or a social movement that seeks to bring a major change in society.

technology (tek-NAH-luh-jee) Methods that use science to solve problems and the tools used to solve those problems.

violence (VY-luhnts) The use of bodily force to hurt, harm, or destroy.

INDEX

A
Americans with Disabilities Act, 26
Australia, 10, 15

B
Banda, Memory, 13
Brazil, 20, 21

C
climate change, 24, 25

D
Declaration of Independence, U.S., 6, 7
discrimination, 14, 15, 18, 21, 22

E
ethnicity, 20

F
Finland, 10
France, 7, 22

G
gender, 4, 12, 13, 14

I
India, 25

L
LGBTQ community, 14, 15

M
Malawi, 13
Mangat, Hana Kaur, 23

N
New Zealand, 10, 11
Norway, 10

P
Pandey, Ridhima, 25
Pataxó, Hamangaí, 21

R
race, 4, 16, 18, 19
racism, 18, 19
religion, 4, 20, 22, 23
Roosevelt, Eleanor, 9
revolutions, 7

S
Saudi Arabia, 11
Sikh Kid 2 Kid, 23
South Africa, 18
suffrage, 10

U
United Nations (UN), 8, 9, 22
United States, 9, 10, 18, 26

PRIMARY SOURCE LIST

Page 8
President of the Council Vincent Auriol delivers the opening speech at the third assembly of the United Nations, Paris. Photograph. September 22, 1948. Getty Images.

Page 9
Eleanor Roosevelt. Photograph. FPG/Staff. January 1, 1948. Getty Images.

Page 21
Activist Hamangaí Pataxó. Photograph. Salvatore Di Nolfe. December 10, 2019. Young Activists Summit in Geneva, Switzerland. Keystone via AP Images.

WEBSITES

Due to the changing nature of Internet links, PowerKids Press has developed an online list of websites related to the subject of this book. This site is updated regularly. Please use this link to access the list: www.powerkidslinks.com/SOOF/equality